"I have known John Fischer for a long, long time. As a matter of fact, I've known him a lot longer than he has known me. I was first introduced to John and his music when my church youth group performed his musical *The New Covenant*. John's work had a huge impact on my life, and like most young Christians growing up in the early seventies, 'All Day Song' was a standard for me and my friends. That song, like the message of the gospel, is simple yet profound. John wrote a song that is familiar the first time you hear it—to me, the mark of an exceptional work. How exciting to see the impact it continues to make, decades after it was first penned."

—**Michael W. Smith,** singer/songwriter

"John Fischer continues to be a voice reminding us that the gospel is true and our lives will be different because of it. In music, and written word, he has invited us into an honest expression of a life lived as a prisoner of hope and a servant forever captured by grace, love, and beauty."

—**Dan Haseltine**, singer/songwriter, Jars of Clay

"Over the last thirty years, John Fischer has helped thousands understand the basic truths of God's love. *Love Him in the Morning* continues to remind us 'He's always got time for you.'"

—**Denny Rydberg**, president, Young Life

"The 'All Day Song' ('Love Him in the Morning') started a genre of music that celebrated Christ in a contemporary way. This book reminds us that John Fischer is still leading us in that same celebration, gently and honestly. This is a refreshing work from a familiar friend."

—**Margaret Becker**, singer/songwriter

"I had no idea 'All Day Song' was penned by John Fischer, and I've known the song for years! The melody alone brings back great memories for me, and John's stories and insights breathe new life into the simple words. There is much to be gleaned from this little book."

—**Fernando Ortega**, singer/songwriter

"If John 3:16 is a constant, then there must be a thousand ways to sing about it. The 'All Day Song' long ago linked arms with 'Jesus Loves Me,' 'O How I Love Jesus,' 'Great Is Thy Faithfulness,' 'There Is a Redeemer,' on and on throughout the centuries-long reach of Christian thought. John Fischer again joins this ageless loveliness with *Love Him in the Morning*. Over the coffee and bagels of our ever-so-ordinary days, John joins us with winsome advice and believable experience."

—**Harold Best**, author of *Unceasing Worship* and *Music through the Eyes of Faith*, and dean emeritus of Wheaton College Conservatory of Music

Love Him
in the Morning

Also by John Fischer

Love Him
in the Morning

Reflections on God's Faithfulness

John Fischer

Revell
Grand Rapids, Michigan

Published by Fleming H. Revell
a division of Baker Publishing Group
P.O. Box 6287, Grand Rapids, MI 49516-6287
www.bakerbooks.com

Printed in the United States of America

Library of Congress Cataloging-in-Publication Data
Fischer, John, 1947-
    Love Him in the morning : reflections on God's faithfulness
/ John Fischer.
        p.   cm.
    ISBN 0-8007-1858-5 (hardcover)
    1. Spirituality. 2. Trust in God. 3. God—Promises. I. Title.
BV501.3.F575 2004
242—dc22   2004003800

To the memory of Horton and Edna Voss,
in whose home the "All Day Song" was written,
and to their surviving children

Contents

Love Him in the morning
  when you see the sun arising;
Love Him in the evening
  'cause He took you through the day.
And in the in-between time
  when you feel the pressure coming,
Remember that He loves you
  and He promises to stay

When you think you've got to worry,
  'cause it seems the thing to do;
Remember He ain't in a hurry.
  He's always got time for you.
So...

John Fischer
All Day Song - 1972

Foreword

I remember my roommate telling me about an amazing artist he had just heard at his Christian university. Rich was impressed at the "real-life, nonchurchy" approach of this bespectacled countercultural singer/songwriter with the funny hair and funky sandals. It was the early seventies, and the Jesus Movement was in full bloom. We lived in Southern California, the movement's epicenter, and the guy Rich spoke of was one of the very first of a new generation of contemporary Christian artists—and was having a seismic impact on my generation.

His name: John Fischer.

Just a couple of years later, I was producing a daily contemporary Christian music radio show in the Los Angeles area when the album *Still Life* was released. It was full of great songs, making it one of the best of the year. But one song in particular caught my ear. It was infectious, easily singable, and left everyone who heard it feeling uplifted and hopeful.

It was the "All Day Song," of course, and our listeners loved that record. We played the grooves off of it.

For the thirty years I've known John Fischer, he has been impacting the lives of my generation and the next through his music, his writing, and his speaking. For more than twenty years he wrote a regular column for *CCM* magazine, and I still don't know how he managed to come up with new ideas month after month.

I've encountered countless people who have told me that John's writing played a key role in their spiritual formation. I love seeing God's gift manifested in such a clear and powerful way.

But back to this song: The greatest testimony to any writer, especially a songwriter, is to create art that stands the test of time. In today's culture of "throwaway" music, a song that endures is a rare and remarkable thing. So here we are, thirty years later, and the "All Day Song" is as relevant and meaningful as ever. And now it is made even more meaningful through this insightful exposition on the lyrics by the songwriter himself. Through this little book, the song is made new again and its message even more powerful. It won't take you all day to read it, but you'll be loving it forever!

John Styll, president, Gospel Music Association;
founder and former president,
CCM Communications, Inc.
Nashville, Tennessee, July 2004

1

Morning

Love Him in the morning
when you see the sun arising;

I woke up to sunlight streaming in on buttery walls. It was a winter morning in January, which in Redlands, California, translates into crisp, clean air with a tinge of frost on roofs where the sun hasn't crept and cold, ripe fruit on the orange trees just outside the second-story guest room window. I was in my early twenties, staying with friends while recording some of my first songs.

This particular day might have been the only day in my life that I could wake up and write this song. Earlier, I might not have had the confidence to try. Later days would be laden with the responsibilities and worries of adulthood—days when I would need to be comforted by the simple truth of my own lyrics. Like the ripe fruit outside, the song was ready, and I picked it. And even then I did not know what I had. The words and the music both came so fast.

I wrote it all down before going downstairs for coffee. I had been working on a Moody Blues guitar riff, which I happened to forget that morning. But whatever I tried to remember turned into something else—they call this accidental creativity—and soon I was singing:

> Love Him in the morning
>   when you see the sun arising;
> Love Him in the evening
>   'cause He took you through the day.
> And in the in-between time
>   when you feel the pressure coming,
> Remember that He loves you
>   and He promises to stay.

I am, as they say, a morning person. On most days now I beat the sun up. Somehow I feel ahead of the game that way, as if I got a jump on everyone else. I used to carry around a poem that depicted all of creation in the predawn hours on pins and needles, waiting to see if, in fact, the sun would rise again. The world was in its infancy, with everything untested, even the idea of a new day. The poem captured that moment right before dawn when the world holds its breath and then bursts into thunderous applause as the first rays of light crest the horizon. "By Jove, he's done it again!" the creatures and all nature cry.

This is the feeling I had that morning with the sun brightening up an already yellow room. He's done it again! He's made a new day and put me in it! What a moment! What an opportunity! Bless the day! Bless the season of my life that has afforded me this luxury! And bless the couple who provided me this luxurious yellow room in which to wake up warm and enjoy all these blessings!

Indeed, the season was a luxury. I had the luxury of time. I was in my young single adulthood, following the good urges of my soul, like the urge to learn—to study the Bible and find out all I could about a faith I grew up with but was just coming to own—and the urge to create—to let my soul express itself in love of God and truth. The urge to free the song that had been buried so long in traditionalism and archaic religiosity. The urge to be in the middle of a movement that was bringing a fresh understanding of Jesus to my generation and to me. The urge to take advantage of a spiritual revolution that felt, to many, like the last gasp of a weary world for God.

My hosts, Horton and Edna Voss, lived with a wealth, a flair, and a generosity that are rare even among those with greater means. "There's more where that came from," Horton often said with a twinkle in his eye, and he meant it about everything in life and faith. I was the auspicious recipient of their unorthodox freedom and generosity—too young and too arrogant to notice how rare it was, but I have noticed it many times over in hindsight.

I grew up with what was more the norm of the day in evangelical Christian circles—a guilt-ridden, tight-lipped Christianity that had to apologize for the enjoyment of anything but a good sermon. Horton and Edna lived well without apology, right down to the two Jaguar XKE's in the garage, matching in everything but color. It wasn't right that only he had his silver dream car, so he got Edna a green one. Of course that left the white '57 Thunderbird for me to drive around town whenever I visited. These people had a love of life and a love for God that were not a contradiction.

At this time in my life, I was young, eager, free to explore the creative gifts I had received from God, and doubly grateful to have an immediate outlet for them. With a Jesus movement dawning and only a handful of people expressing it musically, what I was creating was in big demand. I was on the cusp of a wave that would soon turn into a tsunami.

Oddly, in this song I spoke of worry at the most worry-free time of my life. That proves something about intuition, for it came from a part of me that knew what I would need down the road a bit. As it turned out, a lot of other people needed it too.

The greatest insights always seem to come from the simplest of things. Here those things are the parts of a day: the morning, the evening, and everything in-between, which, if you haven't noticed yet, leaves nothing out.

This is precisely why I decided to call it the "All Day Song." It was simple, it was catchy, and the song was just the kind of thing that might stick in someone's mind for some time. We all carry around useless trivia from popular culture like annoying parasites anyway. Sometimes these things come as slogans or jingles designed to keep us unconsciously aware of some brand of product. And then there are pop songs that lodge in the brain and play nonstop. (I remember once running a whole day on "You're So Vain" by Carly Simon. Undoubtedly true, but did I need to be reminded of it all day?) Or maybe it's some visual connection. Almost every time I shave, I am reminded of a scene from one of Mel Gibson's *Lethal Weapon* movies in which Danny Glover is teaching his son how to shave. "Go with the grain," he says as he pulls the razor down over his face and neck. "Always go with the grain." No wonder I had razor burn for so long. I hadn't had a course on shaving from Danny Glover.

So I thought, if all these stupid things can manage to stay stuck in my mind, why not write something I wouldn't mind having there—something that would help me focus on the right things all day long? Couldn't that work with a song? Well, apparently it has, as the "All Day Song" has become, over the years, my best-known song. Just last weekend a woman walked out of the room when I started singing it in church. She told me later she was so overcome with emotion that she had to leave for a moment. She had not heard the song since the seventies, and so many memories of her early days of faith came rushing back all at once that she could not control herself.

And then there's the balding Chicago businessman—a brand strategy coach for CEOs—who told me recently that he suddenly found himself singing this song as he walked down Michigan Avenue. He hadn't heard it in years, and suddenly it was on his mind. In fact, when I met this man, he treated me as a luminary, and regardless of what I did or told him about myself, I could not shake my celebrity status. While we were having dinner, he even got out his cell phone, called his wife, and broke the news to her about who was sitting next to him. She said, "Tom Petty? James Taylor? Who? No. Not *the* John Fischer! Oh my goodness, get his autograph!"

I looked for signs that this was just a big tease from him—a little charade for my benefit—but it was not. This simple little song has this kind of effect on people.

It's beyond me.

The stripped-down version of this song's chorus could be stated simply as "Love him . . . and remember that he loves you." That's the crux of it. This is all about a relationship. True spirituality boils down to a relationship with God. It's not about going to church, or studying the Bible, or praying the prayer, or chanting the words, or singing the worship songs. It's about knowing God—about loving and being loved. Religion is the furthest thing from it.

When it comes to religion, we have a tendency to make things much too complicated. And I think I finally understand why: We complicate faith because we want to be in control. Keep it just complicated enough so that I feel like I'm accomplishing something with all my religiosity. Keep it complicated so that I think I can do something to earn God's approval. That's religion.

Faith—just believing God for who he is and what he says—seems too easy sometimes. But that's his call.

Religion is complicated. Faith is simple. Jesus said the faith of a child would get you into heaven, and the faith of a mustard seed could move a mountain. Maybe that's why for some people this song has become a lullaby—something associated with a childlike faith. I like that sentiment—the child, the mother's arms, the song, the comfort, the intimacy . . . the relationship. It's all about the relationship.

What are we here for? What is the purpose of our existence if it isn't to love God and enjoy him forever? Every other pursuit wears off in time—not that we don't have other pursuits that are important, but this one outlasts all the others and puts them all in their place. That's why we love him in the morning. When we love him first, we get ourselves in order. This is such a simple thing, and that is probably why it is so easy to overlook. But when we forget to love him first, we lose our center, and all kinds of things that were never meant to hold us break apart in our grasp.

The morning always holds a promise. No matter how bad it's been, it can get better. It's like opening day at the ball field with every team tied for first. As the day moves on, our options narrow until time runs out on every single one of them and we close the book on our hopes and dreams at least for that day. But in the morning it starts over. We don't wake up where we ended; we wake up in a new place. The sun is on the other side of the sky. It hits things from another angle. Everything looks different in the morning's light. We have renewed energy to attack the things that almost crushed us just hours earlier.

"And in the morning you will see the glory of the LORD" (Exod. 16:7). The sunrise is like the glory of the Lord. It reminds us of God's faithfulness. It renews our strength. It gives us a fresh start and a new light on things.

I live in a beach community in Southern California where hills slope down to the sea. Since the sun has to come up over those hills, the day is quite light before I ever actually see the sun. It hits the tops of the clouds hugging the shoreline first. Then it strikes my neighbor's roofline and works its way down, adding deeper tones to the gray shingled siding. The sun brings dramatic color to whatever it touches—color you don't notice as much further into the day because everything is bathed in direct sunlight. You notice more when you can see the contrast with what is still steeped in shadow. One reason the morning is a good time to remember about God: Perhaps we can see the truth more clearly then.

It is good to love him at the beginning of the day, because our love is not predicated on anything happening that day. We are not waiting to see how the day turns out to decide whether we will award God with love and worship. He has already done everything necessary to earn our love and gratitude. And had he done nothing, he would still deserve our praise, even if only for the self-evident fact of who he is as Creator and who we are as part of his creation.

God spoke his pleasure in his Son, Jesus, at his baptism, before his Son ever did anything. It was the sign of a relationship that existed before the world began. Connecting with God at the start of a day is a little like this. It reminds us that we bring pleasure to God even before we do anything.

> When all the people were being baptized, Jesus was baptized too. And as he was praying, heaven was opened and the Holy Spirit descended on him in bodily form like a dove. And a voice came from heaven: "You are my Son, whom I love; with you I am well pleased."
>
> Luke 3:21–22

We too have a relationship with God that doesn't depend on what we do or don't do but simply on who we are as his children. We have nothing to earn and nothing to prove. We can't do anything to gain his approval, and we can't do anything to send it away. Not only are we loved, but God is pleased with us like he is pleased with his Son.

This is why we can love him in the morning. It all begins here. It will end here too at the end of the day, but for now I am thinking about the beginning, and a yellow room, and a song that assures us of his presence and his attentiveness to us the rest of the day and night. And though the room I wake up in now is off-white, it can, like your room—like any room for that matter—contain the presence of God. In the morning, it is good to love God. "Because of the LORD's great love we are not consumed, for his compassions never fail. They are new every morning; great is your faithfulness" (Lam. 3:22–23).

2

Evening

Love Him in the evening
'cause He took you through the day.

The sun goes down on another day. This in itself is a certain grace. No matter what you think, it can't be stopped. The day is done, even if our projects are not. If the day didn't shut down, we might not either. We might just burn out in a ball of flame like the sun dying in the west never to rise again.

But the sun goes down. The stock market closes. The banking day ends. Parking garages empty, freeways swell and then subside for the night. The inevitability of this

29

is a small, daily salvation. This is God's way of saying it's time to stop, take stock of the day, make an agenda for tomorrow, close the books, and be with those you love.

The end of the day is a kindness as much worth celebrating as the beginning. Even the sun goes down in a greater blaze of glory than it usually arises in. The beginning is full of possibility; the end is all about closure. Whatever has or has not been resolved has to be put to rest anyway, if only for the night. If you stop in midsentence, you still stop. Heads go down on pillows. Everything that is there tonight will be there in the morning. Evening is the celebration of the irrevocable—daily closure as darkness falls.

This is the "after" of the morning's "before."

It is no less legitimate.

From this vantage point, God got us through the day. We may not have been conscious of his presence all the time, but he was there nonetheless.

God's faithfulness is especially welcome at the end of the day, when we are often beset by a good deal of regret.

We typically ask more of a day than it can deliver, so it's rare that we end a day without coming up short on something. But this kind of regret is nothing that can't be corrected by raising the bar on our efforts or lowering it on our expectations.

The more difficult regrets are over the things that are hard to undo—things that harm us, others, and God, like regret over lapses in character, dysfunctional behavior, addictive sin, or getting caught in the rut of what we should be free of. This is when we regret what we could have avoided because we know better. We've been here before. We've looked back on too many days and vowed we wouldn't return to this place, yet here we are again.

This is unavoidable because regret is part of the human condition, part of the fall. We all have regrets, because we all have the knowledge of good and evil yet cannot bring ourselves to do good all the time. If we knew only evil or only good, we would not have any regrets, but since we know both good and evil, we are forced into a position in which the good regrets what the evil has done.

I am reminded of something my son came up with when he got caught in his first bald-faced lie. When his mother questioned him on how he could have done such a thing, the wheels in his little four-year-old brain started turning, and the clever guy created a story on the spot to try to save his hide. He said, "You see, Mama, there are these five bugs in my head—two good bugs and three bad bugs. Well, what happened was . . . the three bad bugs took over when the two good bugs went out to lunch."

My son's little story is not far from the truth. Even his numbers, with the good at a disadvantage, seem intuitively human. The apostle Paul says it in a more sophisticated way in Romans 7, but the meaning is pretty much the same: "When I want to do good, evil is right there with me. For in my inner being I delight in God's law; but I see another law at work in the members of my body, waging war against the law of my mind and making me a prisoner of the law of sin" (Rom. 7:21–23). The apostle's bad bugs are definitely giving him a bad time here.

Still, this shows something positive about regret. It means the good, and the desire to do it, is still present. This is part of the redemptive aspect of regret. If anything, it helps us recognize the truth about ourselves and ushers us into God's grace. As long as we think we can pull off this spiritual life—as long as we think God is lucky to have us on his team—we will be unqualified for the grace of God. It's in our *regret* that we throw ourselves at the mercy of God at day's end and receive the love, acceptance, and forgiveness we so desperately need precisely because we haven't lived up to expectations. This is a daily requirement because sin is a daily condition, for which grace is the daily antidote.

Regret reduces us to unconditional love. Grace requires a certain helplessness. Here I've done the best I can do, and it still isn't enough. It never will be. And suddenly I get it. I get that God's love is not because of anything in me or anything I've done or will do when I get my act together someday. Grace is being reduced to my lowest denominator and knowing I am loved even then.

So I come to the end of my day as one who has regrets and yet has the grace to live with them. I remove my soul at night like a cloak that I lay at the foot of my bed. And in the morning I will put it on clean. I marvel that God will have actually gained some pleasure from me today, if nothing else right now as I lie here exposed, loved, and loving him.

I have some remorse over what God had to drag around today, and yet he took me on. He took me through it. He even led me. This is the big part of faith—his faithfulness even in light of my faithlessness. This is the surprise, when God goes beyond just getting us through the day and uses us along the way in the lives of others.

Even if in my estimation I didn't accomplish anything with my day, God did. God accomplished everything he set out to do with my life today. And chances are some of it involved me in ways I won't know for a long time. Second Corinthians 2:14 says that God always leads us in triumphal procession in Christ. That *always* is a key word. In the context of the verse, Paul alludes to a less-than-perfect day of his own, when the Lord had opened a door for the gospel in a new city and yet Paul was so anxious over not being joined by brother Timothy as planned that he left that place and went on to the next town (2 Cor. 2:12–13).

That's when he writes, "But thanks be to God, who always leads us in triumphal procession" (v. 14). The conjunction *but* is the tip-off. This thankfulness he's talking about is juxtaposed to his situation. What he is really saying is "Thanks be to God anyway. He is leading me in triumph even when I miss opportunities he created—doors he opened."

In other words, some days we feel like we shouldn't be thanking anybody for the day, but God's purposes run alongside our real life and are sometimes undisclosed. I'm doing one thing, God may be doing another. I may not understand it all, but I can say at the end of the day that he took me through it regardless. This is not about excusing anything; it is about recognizing God's presence and purposes in my life at all times. Some days it may be hard to say that God took me through it, but in the end, we will all find out that he did.

I think loving God in the evening is in some ways more significant than loving him in the morning. You love God in the evening simply because you love him. In the morning we always seem to have an agenda. We have a tendency to tap into God because of what we want from him for that day. We have ulterior motives. We have requests. We have plans. We need direction. We need resources. We have things we want him to bless. That doesn't leave us a lot of time for reflection in the morning.

We come to God in the morning asking for protection, blessing, and more territory. At night we are less territorial, more apt to want to thank God that he is making sense of all this and to seek him for his presence alone. The day has played itself out. Most of our choices have been spent. If we spend time with God now, it's more out of want than out of need.

> By day the LORD directs his love,
>   at night, his song is with me—
>   a prayer to the God of my life.
>
> Psalm 42:8

Here the psalmist seems to agree with me. For the day, God's love is directed on the psalmist's behalf. At night, his prayer is a song to the source of his being. The day seems to be about ways and means, the night more about worship. In the morning I need direction; at night I receive assurance and give thanks.

"Let the saints rejoice in this honor and sing for joy on their beds" (Ps. 149:5). Now. At the close of the day. When things are stripped down to their basic elements. Now is when I find out if I truly love him. At least, that's the way it is for me. If I have no interest in God at the end of the day, then I might want to give some thought to whether I'm just using him. In the evening, I love him because I want to be with him. God is not the means to an end; he is the end. Soon all that is current in my life will fall away, and I will be left alone with God. How I feel about this is a good test of my relationship with him.

Jesus once healed ten lepers, and only one came back and thanked him. They were all crying out to him, I'm sure, in their sickness and pain, just like we do. But they went on their way, without even acknowledging the miracle, once the pain was relieved. My guess is those lepers were more God-conscious when they were crying out than when they were well. Acknowledging God at the end of the day is a way of coming back and thanking him for hearing me. As the psalm says, "I thought about the former days, the years of long ago; I remembered my songs in the night" (Ps. 77:5–6).

I had a special place to go and watch the sunset years ago when I had time for such things. It was on a cliff over the Pacific Ocean near Santa Cruz, California. I even had my regular spot where the rock made a natural chair for my back against the cliff's edge. Wildflowers bloomed out of cracks in the rock around me, and at high tide the water would crash into the cliff and swirl and churn a hundred feet below.

From there the sunset was like a play—a slow curtain coming down on the day with a blaze of glory for a finale. But God's sunsets use real clouds, water, seagulls, seals, a huge ball of fire ninety-three million miles away, and an atmosphere to move all these elements around in, and they are constantly in motion, though from so far away the sight can appear like a still photograph.

The sunset is God's closure on the day, his way of saying, "I was with you all along, and this is my comment on the day. See how I ended it? Beautiful, isn't it?"

Two of the novelist's most important tools are inevitability and surprise: inevitability in that we know what is going to happen; surprise in that we don't know exactly how. We are seeing the pieces coming together. We are getting pulled into the story, and we will be greatly disappointed if we are wrong. We don't know how the storyteller is going to get us there, but he'd better deliver us safely. Along the way we can relish all the unexpected twists and turns that keep us locked in a good story if we know we can trust the writer for the inevitable conclusion. Still, the possibility that it might not turn out as we expect has to be there too; otherwise we may not believe the ending. We will feel manipulated and patronized.

Here we are once again at the sunset. We knew it was coming, but we couldn't have been prepared for how it is today. Some days we can't see the sunset for all the clouds, but we know, somehow, it's there. It's inevitable.

38

Evening

The story, the world, our lives, the day, all scroll up at some point with the same message: THE END.

And just as God was in the beginning, God will be in the end. *In the beginning, God . . .* is the way it all started, and when you think about it, it will end the same way: *In the end, God . . .* He is Alpha and Omega—the end as much as the beginning. He is on either side of our lives, and on either side of our day. He brackets it with his love. I can lay myself down knowing he is here. And though I close my eyes in sleep, he never sleeps. His eye is always on us and always open.

My mother would often recite a favorite poem about the sunset. She would inevitably tear up in the telling of it. The rest of our family ridiculed her for this because we are people who do not know what to do with our true feelings. We laughed at her, I think, because we were too afraid to cry—afraid of what that might reveal of our real selves. I have thought of that poem numerous times since she passed on. I may have rolled my eyes as she started into it, but all kidding aside, I listened through hidden tears of my own. What I wouldn't give to hear her recite it again. Still, I am grateful she deposited it into my memory bank. I will always hear her voice when I read these words. It's a wistful, vulnerable voice—like one great sigh at the end of the day.

I'm so glad God takes every worn out day and burns it up in sunset. The little mistakes, the futile triumphs, and the petty cares are gathered into one bonfire that bursts into flame against the banks of sky.

I think that God sweeps up the frayed-out ends of day and says, "Poor foolish children. This the spoil of all their goods. When will they learn the way? But since these things are done, we might as well make one great conflagration of it all."

I think He likes to see it burn and stands beside it 'til the last gray ashes fall. Then, across the fretful thoroughfares, over the troubled roofs and petty wars, out of the lonely heights of the unknown, a clean wind blows, all tangled up with stars.

3

In-Between

And in the in-between time
when you feel the pressure coming,

At a music and songwriting camp in the mountains of Southern California sometime in the late 1970s, two high school girls rushed up to me and giggled their way through some goofy hand motions they had just made up for the "All Day Song." At the next general session, I had them come up and teach the motions to the whole camp. The rest is history. Well, maybe it's not important enough to be called history, but in the relatively short thirty-year life of this song, these hand motions have had a hand in spreading the song's message around the world.

That this kind of thing would originate at camp is appropriate. Hand motions are a staple for camp songs, and I often joke about where old John Fischer songs go to live out their days: They go to camp.

A song I wrote in the 1960s, for instance, includes the lines, "Touch someone near you in love, if you can / Give all you have and be part of God's plan," upon which everyone tries to touch as many people around them as possible. Young Life camps have even made this into a game in which the leader calls out a number for how many people they have to touch while they sing that line. Imagine the bedlam "Twenty-three!" would create.

The hand motions to the "All Day Song" begin with arms crossed. One forearm is slowly raised, pivoting on the elbow to a 90-degree position as the first line about the sun rising is sung. For the next line about the evening, the hand then continues on over until the arm is out parallel to the ground, palm up, the sun symbolically having passed through the half circle of its daily arc. Then comes the in-between time when you feel the pressure coming. For this the hand snaps back up to a 90-degree position and waves back and forth, indicating not only the "pressure" but how much of a day this in-between time can cover for most people.

Every time I teach these hand motions, to any age group, in any setting, everyone groans and laughs at the in-between time. They do this, I believe, because they realize that most of their day is spent in-between, and hearing this celebrated in a song, I'm sure, is a great relief.

The "in-between time" is the real reason I wrote this song. It's what I thought I could add that hadn't been said before. Numerous songs and hymns have been written about the morning ("Morning Has Broken" and "When Morning Gilds the Skies") and plenty about the end of the day ("Day Is Done," "Day Is Dying in the West"), but I can't think of one specifically about the in-between time. The mere fact that it acknowledges a pressure-filled in-between time gives everyone who sings it permission to have one. And everyone does.

But more than admitting a difficult in-between time or giving permission for it to exist is the celebration of it. This celebration is laughter in the middle of our unfinished business. This is what I have to thank those high school girls for. They were not so silly after all; they understood what the song was really saying. They danced on the sacredness of the finished product and brought God and joy to the in-between.

How much time does it take to see the sun rising? Not very much. A few minutes at the most. How much time does it take to notice that the day is coming to a close and thank God for taking you through it? Not very much. A few minutes at the most. So where does that leave the in-between? It leaves it filling up the bulk of the day. Not that we feel pressure all the time, but I bet for most of us, it's hard to find a waking moment when we can't find a pressure-related thought close at hand.

Between a rock and a hard place . . .

Between the question and the answer . . .

Between the problem and the solution . . .

Between the prayer and the healing . . .

Between every step of the five steps to victorious living . . .

Between the beginning and the end . . .

In-between the morning and the evening . . . this is where we all live most of the time. If our faith does not meet us in these times, then our religion is, for all practical purposes, pretty useless.

Faith is for the in-between time if it is for anything at all. What good is faith if it doesn't take us through everything? What good is a relationship with God if it doesn't provide something to hold on to when everything around us gives way? If we had the answers to all our questions and the solutions to all our problems, we would have just that—answers and solutions. What if we had no answers but a hold on God that won't let go no matter what? Then, I would argue, we have something worth all the treasure in the world.

I recently sang and spoke at a church in Oakland, California. Before I got up to sing a song for the offertory, the pastor interviewed one of the church's missionaries who was home from his field in Africa. He was not your "typical" missionary. He was a little loud, a little brash, and a little overweight. He spoke of himself as being the most unlikely sort to be a missionary, and the reaction welling up from those in the congregation who had known him since he was a teenager seemed to confirm that assessment. But then he spoke of the amazing grace God gave him to lead to the Lord six teenagers who came to his door and of how a church of two hundred believers mushroomed from those six kids and their families and friends.

At the end of the interview, the pastor brought up a very painful aspect of the past year as he referred to the death of the missionary's oldest son in an industrial accident, how hard that had been, and how much the church still grieved with the father in this tragic loss. The pastor was giving the missionary and the congregation one more time to grieve together. This was obviously not something any of them were ready to put behind them yet. And so I felt a heaviness of heart as I got up to sing.

I had planned on singing the "All Day Song," but the immediate change in the mood made me question my choice for a moment. Was it too simple of a song? Too lighthearted for the mood? After all, this is a camp song, with *hand motions,* no less. Somehow I knew that I was supposed to sing it anyway. As I started into the chorus, I saw the missionary's face light up with recognition, and then I saw the tears roll down as we sang about the in-between time and the pressure. And then I saw the joy return as we finished the song, reaffirming God's love for us and ours for him in return.

In-between six young converts and a new two-hundred-member church was this unexplainable death of the man's grown son, a vibrant young man with his whole life ahead of him. These are the great "whys" of the universe—the unanswered questions we all live with. But the words of the simple song were true, and the faith held, and I was once again amazed at how profound these simple ideas are.

Sometimes I forget that Jesus cried out, "Why?" from the cross. Ever think about that? It must be okay to do this. The "Why?" question does not have to indicate lack of faith. It indicates lack of human comprehension. Sometimes even all the right answers (which Jesus obviously knew) don't touch the pain, and "Why?" is the only thing you can say. To me, Christ's "Why?" from the cross translates to something like, "I knew this was coming, and I know what it's for, but I had no idea it was going to be like this!" It's an entirely human cry that does not cancel out faith.

Between the sacrifice and the resurrection . . .

Between the thrill of victory and the agony of defeat . . .

Between the answer and the acceptance of it . . . there is a real hope that carries us through.

Faith is for this. Faith is for the in-between time.

This is why we can celebrate being in the middle. We can worry about the future or we can celebrate the now. We can study what we should be and wonder if we'll ever make it or enjoy who we are along the way. We can look to ourselves for the answers or look to God and enjoy ourselves in-between. We can look back in nostalgia, or forward into dreams, or straight ahead into the reality of someone else's eyes. These are the choices that face us in the in-between time, and the pressures that so often crowd out the experience of it for what it is and is meant to be.

We were made to live, and in our living to enjoy God now and forever. We so rarely experience the point of our existence because we are perpetually on our way somewhere else.

Our worship too often takes us out of and away from the ordinary. We go to church to worship, and in church we find the answers in the songs, in the sermon, in the Scripture, and in the way we act. I'm sure God appreciates this. I'm sure he enjoys our praise and the efforts we go through to make it our best. But I also think he longs, even more, to be invited into what we do as we walk out of church and into the rest of our lives. And the rest of our lives are lived between the answers.

Does being in-between have to inhibit our worship and enjoyment of God? Do we have to have answers to our questions in order to praise him?

No and no.

We can touch the Lord and be touched by him while we are in the middle.

I am often asked what it's like having people recognize my song and start immediately singing along. Well, sometimes it's rather annoying, especially when it catches me not doing what it suggests. Sometimes the song seems like it was written by someone else, in another time zone.

I think of how simple my life was when I wrote this song. How uncomplicated. How fewer things were on my plate then, compared to what I have now. Fewer disappointments. More hopes and possibilities. In truth, the in-between time has grown to where it occupies most of my waking hours. I've been in the in-between time for as long as I can remember. Some call it midlife crisis, which is fine if by midlife you mean everything in-between the beginning and the end. Midlife crisis? I've been in that for about twenty-five years!

I hear this song now, and I hear it as if I'm in a time capsule, as if I had found it in one of those packages they blast off into outer space in case someone from another planet comes across it. I wonder what I would think if I were in an audience now, watching a twenty-four-year-old version of myself singing this song to me. Would I feel condemned? Would I feel regret? Would I be jealous? Would I want to throw something at this guy? I watch this song relate to others—would it relate to me if I were hearing it now for the first time? It would, but the in-between time would carry the day.

The in-between time is not only between morning and evening. It is symbolic of so much of our lives lived between question and answer, conflict and resolution, right and wrong, black and white, the sacred and the profane—and the list could go on and on.

The in-between time is when we're not experiencing the "victorious Christian life." It's when all the spiritual formulas for successful living don't live up to what they promised. The in-between time is when we are waiting for everything to return to "normal"—some preconceived notion we have of the way things should be but hardly ever are.

We are not—nor will we ever be on this side of eternity—finished products. We are in process, and if we are in process, you could say we are in the interminable in-between. Certainly we grow spiritually. We are, hopefully, becoming more and more like Christ. We are learning to overcome old habits and dysfunctions, but in light of the distance between us and perfection yet to travel, at any point along the way, up to and including our last breath, we have a long way to go.

Sometimes I don't accept God's love in the in-between time because I am too busy blaming myself for creating the in-between. And it is true that the pressure of the in-between can often be the result of my own stupidity—my own sin or careless actions. But God is not like our earthly fathers who would be quick to say, "You made your bed, now lie in it." I know about this because I am an earthly father, and I have witnessed my tendency to remove my love from my children when they are being punished, as if loving them would be a way of easing their pain. I want them to experience the full weight of the consequences of their own actions. I want them to do some groveling. No wonder it's natural for me to think that God would leave me alone when I mess up.

Yet God stood in the way of the consequences of my own actions when he died on the cross. That's what the cross was all about—God getting all tangled up in our consequences. It's about God getting messed up in our mess.

But that's why his promise never to leave me or forsake me does not come with conditions. (He doesn't say, "I will never leave you nor forsake you, unless you screw up again, in which case, you are on your own!") He promises to love me to the end regardless of what I do or don't do. God's love for me—his commitment to stick with me to the end—is true, regardless of what I am going through or who caused it. And he will respond to me again and again when I call to him in the in-between time, because I will mess up again and again.

What this really means is that life can be turned into a celebration in the midst of the in-between. It has to be this way or else we will never sing, never love, never enjoy what God has given us in this life. This is what this song is about. It's a song for all day. God's grace allows us to celebrate the process. If we had to wait until the end, we would still be waiting.

Our celebration, therefore, does not need to be around what we are becoming or waiting to arrive at but around a celebration of who we are now and each day—a celebration made possible by God's grace alone. When we remember that he loves us with a love that is not connected to our lovableness or our performance, we can begin to manage the in-betweens of our lives.

"And in the in-between time when you feel the pressure coming . . ." I just realized recently that this is not about pressure but about pressure *on the way.* We're on the verge of it. It's right around the corner. It's coming. In that sense, this admonition is more about fear than pressure. If the pressure is coming, it's not here yet. It's about the anticipation of something bad about to happen. I believe we suffer more from the fear of something happening than we do with the thing itself.

Fears are almost always bigger than the reality causing them. Besides, when the pressure does come, God always meets us with what we need, but usually not before. Before we need it—when the pressure is only "coming"—it is the fear we need the most help with. Our fears shrink the minute we face the real thing. The bigger challenge, as Franklin D. Roosevelt so powerfully stated, is fear itself.

It's easy to see the flaw in fearing the unknown. God always provides for us in times of trouble or temptation, but not until we need it. For instance, God has promised us a way of escaping temptation, but he says that he offers it "with the temptation" (1 Cor. 10:13 KJV). The help comes along with the problem.

Anyone who has read Corrie Ten Boom's *The Hiding Place*, the story of this exceptional Dutch woman's experience in the concentration camps of World War II after her family was caught hiding Jews, remembers the story of her badgering her dad about tickets for an upcoming train trip. Her father would continually restate that she would get her ticket when she got to the station—no sooner. This became the theme of the book as it was the means by which Corrie endured the horrors she would face. To add fear upon fear would have crushed her. But God did not provide for the things that *would* happen; he always provided for what *was* happening, and in this way she was able to survive.

"Dad, where are the tickets?"

"We're not at the station yet, Corrie."

We're always asking God for tickets out of the things that might be, and that is one request he won't fulfill. To be caught in the fear of what might happen is to ask God for the ticket too soon. And Christ has insisted for us not to add tomorrow's troubles to the ones we have today. Today's troubles are enough. To fear the pressure coming is to live in constant fear, because chances are, something bad is always on its way. But faith tells us something good will arrive at the same time, and that is the essence of walking in faith.

By faith Abraham climbed up the hill with his son Isaac, the only living sacrifice he had with him, and when Isaac asked him where the sacrifice was, Abraham could only say, "God will provide." And God did provide, but not until Abraham's knife was raised and ready to plunge.

I wish I had something to show for all the times I've occupied my mind thinking of ways to wiggle out of the bad things that I anticipate might happen to me. This is a colossal waste of time. Not only because I may not have to face these things, but because I'm getting way ahead of God. That's why remembering that he loves me and promises never to leave me is what the last line of the "All Day Song" chorus is all about. All I need to know for the pressure that I will face ahead of me at any time, at any place, is that God is with me now and will be with me then.

"Stuff happens." Christians aren't exempt from this. We need to make some sort of peace with the process. Announcing and celebrating an in-between time debunks the myth of the perfect life and meets us all where we are with a faith big enough to take on whatever is coming down the pike.

So when you feel the pressure coming, enjoy the Lord. I wonder if Abraham enjoyed the walk up the mountain with his son. Was he savoring each moment or fearing what was ahead? God wants our company. If we wait until all future concerns are alleviated, we may never give it to him. He's in no hurry. He's got time for us and longs to spend it with us, and based on our trust in him, we can enjoy the walk.

This truth is what allows celebration to rise above circumstance. I'm always wanting God to change my circumstances; he is wanting me to change my tune. And this part of the "All Day Song" especially would be a good one:

> And in the in-between time
>   when you feel the pressure coming,
> Remember that He loves you
>   and He promises to stay.

4

Remember That He Loves You

> *Remember that He loves you*
> *and He promises to stay*

If we located all the promises of God and analyzed them for what they have in common, I think we could summarize them all pretty well with just one word: *Remember.*

All those promises are based on who God is, what he has done in the past, and what we can count on him for in the future. Since this has already been revealed to us both in Scripture and in history, then what we have to do when threatened with fear and disbelief is recall these things to our mind.

This kind of promise recall is a good way to look at Psalms, one of the most honest and practical books in the Bible. The Book of Psalms is all about remembering. Over and over again, David gets himself into trouble with his enemies or his fears—he even faces depression over his circumstances—and his way out is always the same: He remembers something about God. He remembers:

his loving-kindness
his mercy
his Word
his salvation
his faithfulness
his deliverance
his justice
his compassion
his righteousness
his strength
his watchful eye
his blessing
his protection

All of who we are and are to be is rooted in God and his character, but we are so prone to forget this. So much of what we believe is unseen.

We are more apt to succumb to our more palpable circumstances and real pain inasmuch as they are immediate and unavoidable. Beliefs are in a different realm; they may not always touch the pain. That does not mean they are less true—just harder to find and hold on to sometimes. The things that challenge our beliefs are usually much more obvious than the things that support them.

That's why it takes faith to live a life of faith.

Paul calls faith "the substance of things unseen," but it doesn't always feel that substantial.

This is why we have to continually be reminded about God, and then, once reminded, we need to remember. Remembering implies doing something. You don't just remember for remembering's sake. This is not an exercise in nostalgia. You remember so as to put yourself in a different place or state of mind. When you feel pressure coming, remembering that God loves you and will be with you always is something you apply to the fear like a tourniquet. You stop the bleeding with the truth and wait on God for further instructions.

These two things—God's love and presence—are guaranteed to every believer at all times, regardless of circumstances or feelings. That's why this song can be sung all the time, at any occasion. I have sung it to my dying mother and then later at her funeral. In the first instance, it woke her out of a coma; in the second, it comforted those experiencing a great loss.

Aside from these two indelible experiences, the most unforgettable was an experience I had singing this song to a roomful of recovering alcoholics in Whiting, New Jersey. I often sing and speak at a camp there called America's Keswick. It is a Christian conference center that also operates an alcohol and drug rehabilitation program for men. The program has been in operation for over a hundred years with a success rate so high it began receiving federal funding well in advance of any faith-based initiatives. Whenever I am invited to the camp, I also make it a point to visit the men in the rehab program.

The first time I did this, I was in for a big surprise. We're talking about a pretty unruly group of men. Guys well acquainted with the rougher side of life. Muscular men, many of them liberally tattooed and pierced. Guys who could tear me apart with their bare hands if they wanted to. I was asked to sing them a couple songs and lead them in a devotional thought for the morning. I struggled over what I would sing. It's kind of hard to do heavy metal on an acoustic guitar. Most of the songs I could think of seemed wimpy compared to their lot in life, something I had never experienced. Needless to say, I was thoroughly intimidated.

But then I started to think, it's morning, and if it was any other group, I would probably start out with "Love him in the morning. . . ." Why should these guys get anything different from anyone else? Are they beyond the message and experience of this song? I decided to put my faith in the universality of the inspiration behind the music and message of this song and sing it for them anyway. I was glad I did, because I found them to be, hands down, the most enthusiastic audience I have ever sung for. They were singing with me before I could get around to inviting them. Well . . . *singing* isn't quite right. They were *belting* out the words with their big hefty voices: "LOVE HIM IN THE MORNING WHEN YOU SEE THE SUN ARISING!"

It was almost comical.

I decided, what the heck, since I'm so successful here so far, I'll try the hand motions.

They went bananas. Here I was with a roomful of big scary guys—tattooed muscles bulging out of tank tops—and I was leading them in the hand motions to the "All Day Song."

Later, when I would run into some of them around the camp (they did most of the maintenance work there), they would greet me with the 90-degree position, waving their "suns" frantically and smiling at the in-between time.

At first I was amazed at their reaction, and then I realized why they responded so positively. Most of these guys were experiencing love for the first time in their lives through this program. Not only from those who run it, but from all the Christians who frequented the camp every weekend—Christians from all walks of life, moms and dads, kids, grandparents. These guys had never known such a loving, supportive environment. Few had known any stability. Many of them had already received Christ's forgiveness through the cross, and they were brimming with new life and the joy of salvation. So when I sang, "Remember that he loves you," they knew what that meant. They were experiencing love from God and God's family for the first time, and they were overwhelmed and uninhibited in their response.

That, by the way, is something I have noticed about this song and the reason I still do the hand motions, regardless of the audience. Doing something dumb and silly has an undeniable effect on people. Everyone suddenly becomes childlike. I've seen it soften the hardest cynic. There is comfort in being given permission to act like a child, and having the support of a group around you is essential to the experience. As long as everyone else is willing to make a fool of themselves, people figure they might as well join in.

Truth is like this. It humbles you. If a child can't get it, no one can. Faith that enters heaven is childlike faith. I used to say that if you are too old for the hand motions to a song, you are too old. I still believe that.

People are suspicious of love when all of their training in life has been based on performance. We are suspicious of love because so few of us have been loved unconditionally. It's against our nature to receive this kind of love. We can hear all about God's lovingkindness and grace toward us, but until we believe it and experience it from someone else, we might as well not even try to know God. We are so backward in these things:

We try to earn love over time; God starts with it.

We try to be love-worthy; God says he loves us already.

We try to love; God is love and loves because it is his nature to do so.

We forget God; God never forgets us.

We lose faith; God remains faithful.

We forget these things easily, so we try to remember, and anything that will help us remember is worth using—even a song that you can't get out of your head. So remember that he loves you. Remind yourself. Tell yourself you are loved. Talk to yourself, if need be. David did this all the time; he liked to talk to his soul: "Praise the LORD, O my soul; all my inmost being, praise his holy name" (Ps. 103:1). In statements like this, he was basically telling himself what to do—part of himself talking to the other part. Music is especially good for this. We sing to our souls. Sometimes singing is the only thing our souls will listen to.

Singing to your soul is not just an Old Testament psalm sort of thing. The apostle Paul wrote, "Sing and make music in your heart to the Lord" (Eph. 5:19). Suddenly it occurs to me that singing this little "All Day

Song," and anything else that helps us focus on the Lord, is not just a nice-to-do thing to help us get through the day. Making music in your heart to the Lord is more than a suggestion; it is a spiritual command. It comes right after "Be filled with the Spirit" (Eph. 5:18). It is what happens when you are filled with the Spirit.

"Remember that he loves you and he promises to stay." When I first wrote this song, this was the line I wasn't sure about. Every good songwriter knows what it means to succumb to a cheap rhyme. In the interest of rhyming, we are often tempted to choose a word that fulfills the requirement but weakens the rest of the song because it's not the best word to represent the meaning or the emotion. "And he promises to stay" did the trick on the rhyme, but I wasn't sure about the meaning. Stay? Stay where? When? Sometimes the rhyme weakens the song, but sometimes the rhyme leads to the discovery of something new—a thought beyond my reach at the time. Now I see this as one of the most important parts of the message of this song.

We all know what it is like to have someone important leave. Conditional love leaves. It stays up to a point, but then it finds something unlovely or simply runs out of resources and checks out of the relationship. Most of us have probably been on both ends of this, humanly speaking. We have left and we have been left in a relationship.

I dated a girl in college who had periodic brain seizures. After the first time it happened to her at school, I found out she was in the health center recovering. She refused to let me in to see her. We were in the early stages of a relationship, and she had told me nothing of this. She knew it was inevitable that I would find out and thought that when I did, I would leave, so she found it less painful to simply push me out of her life. She wasn't bitter about this, nor did she have any anger toward me. She expected my departure based on the pattern of her former relationships. It had always happened that way, so she figured out how she could cut her losses and move on.

But it wasn't going to work that way this time. She had already unselfishly shown me an adventure for life and an understanding of who I was becoming that was unlocking some important things in my personality at a vulnerable time in my life. I had received much from her, and I wasn't about to walk away just when I realized I could give something back. So I didn't leave. I fought my way into the health center that night and back into her life. I made her face me, and because of it we were able to continue a relationship on a much deeper level.

She was not unusual in acting out of self-preservation. We all expect the same thing: We will face a time when someone who loves us can't anymore. Something in us or them makes them leave. We are human and fallible. But this is where God breaks in. He refuses to take no for an answer. God never leaves. He promised to stay, and he stays. You couldn't shake him if you wanted to. In fact, he's been with you all along, and he will stay with you to the end. He will finish what he started with each one of us.

I am also reminded of the Samaritan woman Jesus met at the well of Jacob (John 4). At a critical point in their conversation, Jesus revealed to her that he knew all about her sordid past—that she had had five husbands and the man she was currently living with was not her husband. Later when she ran into town to tell everyone she had met the Messiah, she referred to him as one who told her everything she had ever done. She repeated it numerous times. "Come see a man who told me everything I have ever done." Well, not everything, mind you, just the worst things—the things you don't want anyone knowing about if you can help it. And that was the point. Not just that he was a prophet, but that he knew all this about her *and didn't leave*.

He's been with us all the time. When we didn't see him, he was there. He was arranging the things in our life to bring us to the end of ourselves and an awareness of him. And now that he has our attention, he aims on keeping it. He loves us, and he knows that our loving him back is the best thing that could happen to us. So he stays, even in spite of our efforts to escape sometimes.

"And surely I am with you always, to the very end of the age" (Matt. 28:20). This is how the first Gospel in the New Testament ends—with Christ's promise to stay. He leaves us with the promise of his presence at all times, a promise we can call upon at any time and any place. He is with us always.

Actually, God has been saying this to those he loves since the beginning of his relationship with the human race. He told the Israelites, "Do not be afraid . . . for the LORD your God goes with you; he will never leave you nor forsake you" (Deut. 31:6). This promise was first said to Joshua and later applied to all believers (Heb. 13:5).

God stays. No matter what happens, God stays. That means he's with me now, even if I don't feel like it.

He's not going anywhere.

5

Worry

When you think you've got to worry,
'cause it seems the thing to do;
Remember He ain't in a hurry.
He's always got time for you.

I am a chronic worrier. I come from a long line of
German worriers. Not warriors, mind you. *Worriers*.
Left-brained forehead-creasers who have to have an
answer and an explanation for everything. My grand-
father worried himself into a nervous breakdown.
In the mental ward of a hospital, he would spiral

bigger and bigger imaginary circles in the air with his hand until he couldn't make them any bigger, and then he would break down and start all over again. He cracked from trying to care about more than what he could control. Of course, every time he tried this, he came up with the same result. His arm simply wasn't long enough to encompass everything he worried about.

His wife worried too. Maybe even more than he did. Funny, I can't even picture my grandmother smiling or laughing. Her face, and her whole nature, was just permanently fussy. She and my grandfather were first-generation German immigrants who had lived a hard life. However, I can picture my grandfather laughing. He must have mellowed some after his breakdown, which occurred before I came on the scene. He must have figured out how to make peace with what was outside his biggest circle and beyond his reach. Nonetheless, my grandparents' worried nature passed on down to my father, my brother, my sister, and me. Nervous breakdown or not, we are good at drawing spirals in our minds.

"It takes a worried man to sing a worried song," sang the Kingston Trio in my earlier days, which makes me wonder what it must take to write one. A really worried man, I suppose. Well, that's me. I wrote this part of the song because I knew I would need it as much as anyone.

Let's think for a minute about the anatomy of worry. One thing I've found out is that worriers are not action-oriented people. They are not doers. They tend to be thinkers because that is where the worry weed grows—in the mind. Doers are too busy to let the weed grow. Sometimes I actually like being so worried that I can shut down and not have to do anything. This is what I call *worry sabotage.* It's very useful to the worrier as an excuse for inaction and devastating to those around him because nothing gets accomplished.

For instance, one can worry about all the possibilities, dissect them, and, like a giant chess game, try to strategize what to do. If I do this, reasons the worrier, then this will happen, and that will put me over there, and I'm not sure that's where I want to be, so let's back up and try another move and see what happens with that. You know those speed chess games in the park that force you to move within a given amount of time? I should have such a clock on my worry. "Time's up! Make your move or lose the game!"

Doers are less worried because they are eliminating possibilities as they go and also finding new ones they didn't know existed. This reveals part of the futility of worry: You don't even know all your resources, because some of them won't reveal themselves until you start moving. When you worry, you are often applying today's knowledge to tomorrow's problems. That will just keep you stuck in today. God's provisions certainly work almost exclusively in the here and now. God is famous for not giving us what we need until we need it. He usually doesn't even tells us about it in advance.

Faith is an action word. I've heard the term "faith in action." Actually, there is no other faith. Faith is action. Even if faith means waiting, exercising it is still an activity—to wait and not worry. In fact, waiting sometimes makes the greatest demand on faith. We try to figure out what we're going to do before we get there. Worry almost always deals in a future for which I have no answers. Faith deals in the perpetual now. This is why faith and worry don't mix.

Last night I was awakened in the middle of a sound sleep by my daughter calling from an international time zone. She had an immediate problem that I would need to help her solve in the morning. This is the kind of time when worry has a heyday with me. I'm now lying in bed, drawing circles in my mind, trying to solve this problem. And like my grandfather, I keep going back to the beginning and retracing circles until I can't reach any farther. Then I go back and start again, adding to my already compounding worry the fact that I am now missing a good amount of sleep I will need the next day—even resenting my daughter for waking me up. This is an instance when the activity of faith would be to go to sleep. Not an easy thing. At this point, sleep is faith with substance. It's not just words; it's a real presence that calms my nerves and allows me to believe that God is never in a hurry and will give me his full attention later in the day when I really need it. What I need right now, however, is sleep, and based on an active faith, I can sleep.

A spiritual principle is at work here. This isn't just common sense and good psychology, though the principle is probably shared by both. "Work out your salvation with fear and trembling," wrote Paul, "for it is God who works in you to will and to act according to his good purpose" (Phil. 2:12–13).

This is action, but it is God's action in and through me. The interaction of our work and God's work as explained here is somewhat mystical and obscure, but it sounds like God's will and God's work are made known as we act out, by faith, what we believe he has asked us to do. In other words, God works through our work, and that would mean he can't do anything if we don't do something. It's like the old adage about steering a car when it's not moving: You can steer it, but it won't do any good unless it's already going somewhere.

Don't you think that all of us, in general, spend too much time in our own heads? So many books to read, so many sermons to listen to. We do a lot of mental spiraling through all those books and seminars and often get stuck somewhere in the middle of the next thing to do. We worry too much about our next move instead of just making it. Nike gives good advice for most of us: Just do it.

Jesus was always talking about doing. The kingdom of heaven, according to Jesus, is not about sitting around brooding over what to do. It's about doing—looking for lost sheep, cultivating a field, sowing seed, harvesting, buying a field, lighting lamps, investing a talent, throwing a banquet. . . . The kingdom of heaven is like all these things. Jesus was always asking us to interact with the truth and the world around us—to be doers of the word and not only hearers. This is the shortcoming of most from-the-cradle Christians—too much hearing and not enough doing. We've heard it all. We've done so little.

Having said all this, everybody worries at least sometimes. Worry is a basic human reaction to uncertainties in life. Even those who are primarily doers have worries. Worry is mainly the result of our finiteness. It is what we do with what we can't solve: We worry about it.

I'm sure this is why the Bible says, "Cast all your anxiety on him because he cares for you" (1 Peter 5:7). We have to do something with these things we can't do anything with in our minds. Worry is a useless thing, but something still has to be done with it. It doesn't just vanish. God understands this and says, "Throw it over here," or as the psalmist put it, "Cast your cares on the LORD and he will sustain you" (Ps. 55:22).

When worry seems like the thing to do, we've got to remember that God's not in a hurry. He has his own time line and everything is on schedule. God's spirals go out to the ends of the universe. His arm is long; nothing is beyond its reach. No question is unanswered in God's economy, no problem unsolved, no purpose thwarted, no goal unreached. We can't reach or see that far, but when we cast our cares out to him, he can care about them in light of the whole.

Notice neither of these verses says he will remove the cares or their source. They say to rid ourselves of them by rolling them over to him. When we do so, he will sustain us because, most importantly, he cares for us. I've always preferred the way the King James version plays on the caring word: "Cast your cares on him for he cares for you" (1 Peter 5:7 KJV). It's love, and the one loving me, that allows me to give up my worry.

God's not in a hurry. He never panics. People only panic because they have limited time, resources, and vision. God has unlimited quantities of all of these. He stands outside of time, and he has all power and all creation at his fingertips. God's not in a hurry because everything is on schedule. There are no surprises. No monkey wrenches to tie up his works.

It's almost as if he says, "Now that we've taken care of all your worries, what was it you wanted, my child?" At this point we kind of stutter because we never got beyond our worry. We thought the whole thing was about getting over our worries, but it's not. It's about us in relationship with God, about loving him and doing his will in the world —about getting over our worries so we can do something useful and be someone useful in relationship with him. You have to get beyond your worry before you can have a positive effect anywhere.

Something happened a few years ago that got my attention. It was a direct supernatural encounter with God's invisible kingdom. I haven't had many of these. Just two, in fact.

The first was a visitation in my parents' '57 Ford when, as a teenager, I first received the call to write contemporary music about faith. The second was on just a normal day in my home office. I do remember that I was quite stressed at the time. I had even asked God the night before to show himself to me and, of course, expected an immediate response. When I didn't get that, I dismissed the request as foolish and trivial. Sure, faith doesn't need signs to keep functioning. Still . . . it just would have been nice . . .

The next day I was going through my ordinary morning routine when I picked up the phone and dialed my agent in Illinois. An older woman answered the phone. This was my agent's designated business line. No one but he had ever answered this number in five years. "I'm sorry, I must have dialed the wrong number," I said, only to hear the woman on the other end say, "Well, not necessarily."

"What do you mean?" I asked, my curiosity definitely aroused. The rest of the conversation went as follows. I remember every word.

"Are you a Christian?" she asked.

"Yes," I said in amazement.

"Well then, I have a message for you."

"Okay . . ."

"Fret not; God's grace is sufficient; serve him with gladness."

"Is that it?"

"Yes, that's it."

That was the extent of our conversation, and this is how I know this was a supernatural visitation from God: It addressed, right off the bat, my big issue—worry. The message was exactly what I needed, because at that time my worry was robbing me of my creativity, which is the essence of my work. So the message was not only to not worry but also to realize that God would provide and then, with that care aside, to serve him with gladness. The issue went beyond just getting over anxiety; it was about getting unstuck so I could act in faith and produce something useful in his kingdom.

One of my favorite parts of this song is the last half of the verse that reminds us that God is not in a hurry, that he always has time for us. The images are childlike and easy to grasp but not things we usually associate with God.

First, he's not in a hurry. Well, of course not, or he wouldn't be God. The implication that goes along with someone in a hurry is that they are slightly out of control—someone who has committed to too many things and is having to rush from one to the other to get through all their responsibilities. As they do this, they are not giving their full attention to what they are doing. More like skirting on the surface of things so as not to get too entangled or bogged down by any one of them.

Someone gave my wife a little wire sculpture of a frazzled but well-dressed woman with four arms holding a cell phone, a briefcase, a to-do list that numbers into the high sixties, and a sign that reads "best stressed." This is usually what we think of when we think of someone in a hurry.

It's an interesting lesson to read through the Gospel accounts of the life of Christ and try to find any evidence of him being in a hurry like this—like we so often are. It doesn't exist. Even in the press of the crowd, he felt a woman touch him with a need, and he stopped and gave her his attention. He was deliberate about everything he did. He cared personally for the individuals around him yet never lost track of the masses.

Now, of course he was not only human but also God within the limits of his human incarnation, yet he seemed to pull off this unhurried caring with grace and compassion. That's because he is God, and as God, outside of the human limitations of being the Messiah, he can do this for everybody.

He can do it for us. He can pay attention to our most intimate inner need, and this while managing the universe. This is the point of the second part of this phrase: "He's always got time for you."

Like an important father who is never bothered to be interrupted by his children, God can pay full attention to our needs and requests. We can walk right into the boardroom and stop the meeting. He lets us do this because we are his. We are a priority. He has everything else under control; he can listen to his children. At any time we call on him, we have not only his ear but his mind, and his heart, and his whole being turned in our direction.

Impossible? Not with God.

Maybe there was another reason for my grandfather's circles. Maybe he was in too small of a place and he was trying to get out—out beyond his own limited resources. Out where his faith could take on bigger proportions. Out beyond the small places that trapped him in the same fears and the same excuses. Maybe he actually wanted a bigger, more dangerous life, not a smaller, safer one. That "smaller and safer" option has been taken by many, which is a shame since faith seems made for bigger things.

This bigger, more dangerous life was certainly true for the Old Testament heroes from Moses to Malachi. It was certainly true of Jesus and his disciples. It was true of the apostles and the early church. It was true of the martyrs and those who carried Christianity through the dark ages. It was true of the eighteenth-century reformers and the nineteenth- and twentieth-century evangelists. It was even true in the fantasy worlds of Tolkien's Bilbo and Frodo Baggins and Lewis's children in Narnia.

Show me a person whose world is shrinking and I will show you a fearful man with no desire to venture out beyond that which he can control. And I would guess that this person, in spite of a smaller, more manageable world, still finds much to worry about. Maybe even more, because now he has more time to worry.

Faith on the move has little time to worry. You worry when you are waiting to go into battle. You don't worry when your sword is flailing and your shield is flashing in the sun. You are elated. You are drawing on strength you didn't know you had. Frodo Baggins could stay at home and smoke his pipe by a warm fire, or he could save the world. When you think about it, our choices are not that much different.

6

So . . .

There is one more line in this song. It is made up of one word—one insignificant little two-letter word that comes at the end of the verse and doubles the thought back into the chorus. When it is sung, I often pause and extend the note out an inordinate amount of time, making a big deal of it on purpose. In the hand motions, it is visually turned into the word *sew*, and the fingers trivialize it with the mime of needle and thread, but in the song, this little word is far from trivial. It is pivotal. It's what wraps the song around itself and keeps it singing all day.

It's what makes it more significant each time around. It's what turns revelation into something concrete.

There is the morning and evening of a day, and there is also the morning and evening of a life. Nothing captures the latter for me better than a memorable meeting between our six-month-old Chandler and my eighty-nine-year-old mother who had become virtually lost to us from the gradual erosion of her memory. It turned out to be the only time these two would meet and the only words they would exchange in this life.

My mother's deterioration had been gradual, over the course of almost six years. During that time I was surprised to learn how much communication was still possible in spite of the memory-robbing killers of old age. One day I led her over to a piano in the lobby of a nursing home and watched in amazement as she began touching the keys ever so lightly but gaining strength as she went through two fragile pieces by memory. She couldn't recognize her husband or children, but she could play every note of her cherished hymns flawlessly.

During another season she still knew who I was if I called her on the phone, though when we talked all of her sentences would fall off and end up rattling around in the same garbled verbiage. She could not follow any line of thought for more than a few phrases. Nonetheless, I would take notes during these conversations as, through questions and comments, I continually tried to take her back to where she had left off. Without fail, every time that I would hang up the phone after one of these sessions, I would go over the things I jotted down and find embedded there a personal message to me. It was always different and always something I needed.

And then at times I would just sit with her and not say anything at all. I actually think this was when we communicated the most. One of those occasions, at a local arboretum, I captured in a song with the following lyrics:

> On a park bench she sat looking
> At the trees that lined the hill.
> Trying hard to find the words
> When she knows she never will.
> So she watched the sad leaves shimmer,
> All innocent and shy,
> Having lost her dearest memories
> To the colors of the sky.
>
> And I sat there with her, wondering
> (Though she did not know my name)

Love Him in the Morning

If she could see me smiling,
And love me just the same.
And I thought I saw a glimmer
Of all the years gone by,
As I caught the golden sunset
In the corner of her eye.

She didn't have to say it.
Didn't even have to try.
'Cause she said it for a lifetime
From the corner of her eye.

Now she dances by my window,
But I cannot let her in.
Or recreate the feeling
Of her touch upon my skin.
Still I see a ray come shining
From across a broken sky;
Like that gleam of reassurance
In the corner of her eye.

She didn't have to say it.
Didn't even have to try.
'Cause she said it for a lifetime
From the corner of her eye.

Go . . .

On the day my son would meet my mother, Chandler and I arrived at the care center to find that she had been asleep for twenty-four hours. The staff was concerned that she might have slipped into a coma. We walked into her room and found her unresponsive to conversation. So, remembering her experience at the piano, I decided to try singing.

Music was her love second only to Jesus. So I sang her the chorus of the "All Day Song." It was her favorite among my own compositions. I finished the song and asked her if she remembered it.

"Uh-huh," she said matter-of-factly, opening her eyes wide.

I seized upon the momentary lucidity and set Chandler before her, introducing him as her new grandson. She reached out and grabbed both of his hands, like she always did to people. She'd either take you by the hands or, what was worse, if you were a kid, take your face with both her hands, look you straight in the eye, and ask you some pointed question that made you squirm all over. Or quote you a Scripture verse.

This time she looked straight at Chandler and said, "So . . . what are you going to do?"

That was it. Out of the blue, out of a coma, out of wherever it was she had been in for twenty-four hours, she delivered the telling question to a six-month-old, "What are you going to do?"

Well, what could a six-month-old baby do but respond with some gibberish or just stare? He came out with the gibberish and a dash of gobbledygook, to which she replied, as if every word of it were understood by her, as I believe it was, "Well, I'm not surprised!" And that was the end of the matter.

I can't wait until I get to heaven and find out what really did transpire in that conversation. I'm sure they both know, and I'm sure it was profound. Somehow I think a whole lifetime of relationship was bound up in that brief exchange. I believe Chandler received, in some mysterious way, all he would need from his grandmother in that one question: "So . . . what are you going to do?"

What's more, he wowed her with his reply.

As from out of the long sleep of our inactivity, or silence, or long list of excuses, or whatever it was that kept us distant, God speaks the same question to each one of us.

"So . . . what are you going to do?"

What reply will you give? It may be as unintelligible to others in the room as was Chandler's, but it will be known to God and you, and that's all that matters.

And maybe you will surprise him with your answer. Or maybe you won't.

So . . . wow him. Step out in faith and believe who he is and what he said. And as you go, remember to take this little song with you. It's good for the whole day.

So . . .

> Love Him in the morning
>   when you see the sun arising;
> Love Him in the evening
>   'cause He took you through the day.
> And in the in-between time
>   when you feel the pressure coming,
> Remember that He loves you
>   and He promises to stay.

About the Author

Artist and thinker **John Fischer** helped pioneer the genre of contemporary Christian music and was a pivotal figure in the Jesus Movement of the early 1970s, which inspired a new generation for God.

He has recorded twelve albums, and his best-known songs appear in hymnals and songbooks and around many a campfire.

He is the author of seven nonfiction books, including the best-selling *Real Christians Don't Dance*, and four novels, including *Saint Ben* and the recently rereleased *Dark Horse*, an allegory about the Christian life.

He wrote a spotlighted, award-winning column in *CCM* magazine (Contemporary Christian Music) for more than twenty years. He also writes columns for

Chuck Colson's BreakPoint Online (www.breakpoint.org), Walk Thru the Bible's devotional magazine *indeed,* and *Relevant,* a magazine for twentysomethings on "God, Life, and Progressive Culture."

John speaks and sings regularly at churches, retreats, conferences, and on college and university campuses around the country.

John and his wife, Marti, are raising a toddler son in Laguna Beach, California, and have two adult children as well.

Visit John's web site at www.fischtank.com.

Dare to break out of complacency
& live a life of authentic faith.

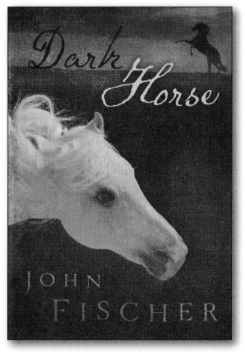